# salmonpoetry

*Publishers of Irish & International Poetry*

# Find A Place That
# Could Pass For Home

## GLENN SHEA

Published in 2010 by
Salmon Poetry
Reprinted in 2021
Cliffs of Moher, County Clare, Ireland
Website: www.salmonpoetry.com
Email: info@salmonpoetry.com

ISBN 978-1-907056-54-3

Cover artwork: Samuel Palmer - *A Hilly Scene* © Tate, London 2010
Cover design & typesetting: *Siobhán Hutson*
Printed by imprint*digital*.net

# Acknowledgements

Acknowledgements and thanks are due to the editors of the following in which some of these poems first appeared:
*Connecticut River Review, Duckabush Journal, Hiram Poetry Review, Maryland Poetry Review, Mudfish, New Stone Circle, Northeast Journal, Parting Gifts, Pearl, Pegasus, Pulsar, Rattapallax, Red Fox Review, Small Pond Magazine, Sow's Ear,* and *Wolf Moon Press.*

Bows and thanks too to Joyce Rankin in Judique, Nova Scotia, to Dan Cianfarini in Cambridge and John Kliphan in Paris, longtime friends and north stars all, whose advice and help have always come in the nick of the spirit's time.

# Contents

Who I am really (and again)
is the youngest son of fable,
who left and came back
different, eyes cauled
with the aftersight of palaces.
Now tell me who you are,
and I'll believe.

# For Peter Fallon

Peter, you found yourself at home
in County Meath, made intricately simple song of it,
and, stranger, I know you, as I have
hunted home myself. Poets are a little lost
here in New England, our souls gypsy south
and the county's heart hardens northwards; find a place
that could pass for home and a week's business'll
whisk it away. Still the land
if nothing else remains; they build over it
but the bones of it peer through, a few cows
and barns stand trim and local, the roads still
hug the coiling weft of the hills, as if the crew
were whiskey when they laid them. Our love
is not made of common work or common dreams,
that's gone, but of our lives and memory being
long enough, rooted enough
to make repeated things a ritual, houses and land
warmly haunted with worn familiars, each road
enough traveled to have been, once, a splendid arrival.
Enough Yankee in the land persists
to be home to those acres of ourselves
that are weathered, stony and intractable.
The other home is made of language,
the maps and messages of other people's
searching, "the noble house of my thought."
I have more of home than most but lose my way
often; Peter, your poems and yourself being
at home in Loughcrew are shelter
to my gypsy part; they are fixed stars,
that send me safely on my own way home.

# For Olga K-Pastuchiv

The wine-dark sea, you called it, the old tag,
and even there, on the continent's blunt edge in Maine,
the word applied; we walked back over moss and fern,
past an egret birch-white in profile against the green
but beyond the downroll of rock the sea there
retained its Aegean hue, seaweed beneath the surface
making it burgundy and dark.  Later in fall, you said,
when leaves in the crevassed rock turned red
they looked like blood, like rivulets running down the stone,
and the dog, made lazy by the sun hot on its fur,
fell asleep, giving you a place to lay your head.
The sea was all my god that day, holding me
in its thought 'til late, when ragged v's of geese
lettered the evening sky; there at land's end the sea
in its responding vastness gave our hearts their image back,
telling us no earth can hold us or be finally our home.

# One

The imprinting of gesture, the memory
of the body:  be thoughtful of these
with the young.  These things stick.
I could wish, for instance, that in
the long bored hours of worship at
St. Mary's I had been taught
not to sit and kneel with bowed
head, as these gestures (though
I harbor them as my child's self,
immute) now seem passive and
self-abasing.  I could prefer I
had been taught to raise (as
I did a few nights ago, at
prayer) my arms above my head,
hands apart and open:  gesture
of beseeching praise, of
poverty, the longing to be
taken up, embraced, all these
not bound in gesture but
inseparable one, the body's
fit apostrophe to blessing.

# The Docks

Wash, gird, shine, polish the sleek city:
still the bay and its reprobate energy
resists.  Still the clog and foam
of garbage bumps the docks, back and
forth, back and forth, in its tight tidal
dance that clings to shore; still the
stubble-faced dirty men in check flannel
shirts loiter at the water's edge, with
anywhere else they could go but
here's where they go; still the slop
gushing up, water and mud on the
rotted wood and the paint on the boats
craggy and split.  A few hundred
yards away the neat town or city
may begin, brushed and courteous,
but still down there on the docks
the Portuguese family is playing the same
music it's always played, on the
faded bumped tarnished instruments
that have seen a hundred cities many
times each, the parents swarthy and
fattish, the boy's face sprouting its
first dark moustache and the sister
not slender and graceful but
bearing a layer of baby fat
and her chunky calf and thigh
never kicking under the tutu skirt
quite high enough in the same old
played and practiced dance to
be amazing but she and the boy
wheel around embraced in the
clothes of the year before, the
blues and reds even muted in
the mist light, like everything
around them, like the line
of the far shore's horizon.

# Henry Higgins and the Divisive Issue of Class

The greased, smutty lumbering train
of thought, audible up the shaft of the stairwell,
its repetition and grind clanking past
the postcard of Akhmatova on the wall
(facing right with her blunt boxer's nose)
the workman's tight influent voice and
its repeated words and the honesty
grunting under it: "He lied," he says,
and those words crawl on their elbows
past the artist's silhouette of Tsvetaeva
(her pointed nose daintier than Anna's)
"He lied. Why did he lie? You don't lie
to get a job!" but he is matter of fact
even in that, the voice at the same
semi-shout, knobbling up the stairs
into the room of what someone called
my Salvation Army furniture, the futon
on the floor, and then downstairs
his watch, his watch, mind you, strikes
twelve, tweedling its startling tin-
glockenspiel tones to the tune of the first
notes of the Notebooks of Anna Magdalena
Bach, and Bach beeps upstairs, his spirit
great even in jest, past the calendar
picture of Anjony Castle, its four turrets
grouped and graceful as they could only be
in France.

# Notre Dame de la Belle Verrière

Impatient again and restless,
I tore my posters down and
postcards and cartoons and
drawings, to make way for what
hasn't happened yet; my usual
torment, all possessions borne
as weight; road-hunger, crossed
with a wish to be domestic,
settled. What I could not
destroy was the card of you,
crowned mother with the dark
child in her lap, blue and red
and white in glass, flanked with
seraphim, the dove above you:
oldest deity of France, the mother
and son, to whom men have
offered their rivers, their wheat
and verse, in whom I have had
so far only an improper and
unsaving faith. Star of the sea,
be help to us, my heart cried.
To tear down such colors
would be an end. So I have
left you in your place above my bed,
altar of lone hours and hope's
thin durance, this loyalty
my prayer, my pauper's coin.

# Peter

We have Peter in our town—or had,
I haven't seen him lately—a prophet chosen
by Jesus, or so recorded in the journals

he kept for a three-credit course
at the local evening classes, the prof
expecting some pages of response

to *Mice and Men*; he recorded instead
his year in the exile of the asylum
during or before which the letter

of Scripture suggested it was time
he pluck his right eye out and
lop off the hand of sensual offense.

I haven't made this up. We see him
in the market, his turvy and socketed
face somber and turned inward,

left hand and stump maneuvering
to deal with wallet and folded
bills or the smooth

and handleless things, the bulk
round weight of watermelons,
everything we haul with two hands,

and Peter, clothed in the question
of literal meaning, the other mind of
doctrine, the local flesh of prophecy.

# The Lovers

As I lay on the table
and you peeled the strips of flesh
off me, you looked puzzled
and said, you're making  something
out of nothing.  Flayed to the guts
in front, I rolled over,
offering you my back, and said,
you're making nothing out of
something.  Okay, you said, if that's
the way you want it.  That's not
the way I want it, I said.

# Rejoinder

Come let us kiss and part,
Drayton said, and good, I said,
for the slight pride of those lines
I understand, the need to say both
a civil word's farewell yet
say with it with a tone that pain
has been dealt and love denied.
Shake hands forever, good too,
formal is final and fair and
decent, we carry our storms
of loss but that happens, love
can be begged but never expected.

But the fainting Cupid you finish with,
who might revive by the kiss
how many times refused; don't give me that.
Give me the stiff bow,
give me the spit of venom if you have to
or the hurried turn away,
but for God's sake don't give me hope.

# Memory

I have been held at gunpoint twice,
a situation so madly passive
that the mind leaps tensed to its feet,
enlarges with rapt attention the second's space
between clock-ticks, scanning
for the unguarded moment in which to act;
but none came for me.  The
second time, the robbery in the shop—
the beersmell and grimesmell of
the man, metalsmell of the gun—
reminded me of the first, being held
at the border of Ulster, our
cards checked, the automatic
in the soldier's hands swinging
toward the children biking in to us
from the sane world of the field.
No not them! I wanted to shout,
but of course no shots were fired;
this was routine.  Tragedy
passed by, intent on others, the accidents
of its going-by leaving a pair of white marks
in memory, blanks, imagining's
witness to what I could not have helped.

# Poet's Son's Death

Did you resent them,
dying before him as you did, the poems,
some of them the most beautiful he ever wrote?
Did you stare at the oddity of your name in print,
unpermitted, the baldly public love
being so insistently heart-wrung and permanent,
there in its purity for the world to see?
Set down there, they were the best of him,
caught, recorded; not his physical
ugliness, his brute drunk rages, his
abandoning your mother, his mistress
and her carnal weekend presences.  No, these
for his readers would be his struggling
with the Muse, his soul-light leaping
with affection towards his son past
the fleshy fences of alcohol and lust.  And you,
lying down there in this dust, who would record
your light, your struggle, your purity?  Who
would set down the daily and suffocating
anger of arguments that print had decided,
ruling against you?  Rest, friend,
in your unsettled rage, that years now will not alter;
leave us our guesses to hazard, your back
turned on our attempts at elegy.

# For Joyce Rankin

i. No news is good news, they say,
and no longer lazy
in concurrence I seek to live
long flowering fields of weeks
without event, my letters lacking
in the usual bait and tackle,
the hasty postscriptum,
the neat box of stanza and event,
to live so simply the river's day
again, its tide and fragrance
empty of incident
that wherever else you are,
fishing words up from the Ness
or basking in Jerusalem's light,
the place I keep for you
will be here, held safe.

ii.   thank you for the postcard
     you're right    I liked it
     so much that in a few seconds
     for a few seconds
     I built a house inside
     the picture   a very old house
     with dark Victorian wood or
     maybe white and bright instead
     if you preferred   where you
     would live with your young man
     and I with mine and
     we would all get along
     on very little (I would say
     this is quite a house) and
     somehow the world
     would not be so much
     with us and our poems
     would be as dewy as the green
     grass is and we could
     walk out in the morning
     to look at the fjord
     which would still be there
     as it is on the postcard
     and the little girl in white
     would be our neighbor
     somehow and somehow
     the light on the linden
     would be always like that

# Revising

The second draft is you at work,
not the bang-nailing away but walking
around the house outside and in,
testing hinges, bumping the sash
to know it'll keep October out,
not exalting but absorbed, hawkeyed
to that barren patch that needs
burning off, tending the fenced circle
of workfire that'll fill itself in
come spring, nothing left but unbroken
arable, good field, the green
soft stems of perception.

# The World is Nothing

By the word of the world it seemed
you never won, John, not coming
or going; a poor childhood at
one end, a blood-coughing death
at the other in Italy, at all
the distance illness and
a foreknowing anguish put
between you and the woman
you loved; the much-mocked
Endymion at one end, and the
abandoned romances, left
to us like turrets and ramparts
with no castle beneath them,
left unendable at the other
and just about every piece
between them mocked by
some critic or other, and one
brother fled to America, and
a sister too young to be
any companion at all, and
your brother Tom pitifully
dead before you:  all
by the world's account
an addition of failures
and leavetakings.  But
glories rested in you, and
world-shouldering braveries,
and words fell through you
onto paper as sweetly
as soft rain, John Keats;
the world is nothing.

# For Ivan Blatny

The tyrants took over: the landscape
grew cracks like a mirror, the birds began
to tell lies, reality grew rifts. You fled.
They reviled you: not just the tyrants, your friends.
They declared you dead on the radio.

In England the tonweight of freedom bent you.
Nightmares of being dragged back grew in the porridge.
You hid yourself in your madness 'til they built
a house around you in the little coast town. You were,
but if no one knew where, you hoped, they might forget.

The poems came, mistaken for ravings. Fought their way
to the window. Were stolen home. Were whispered.
Were gathered. Printed, in deep secret. Printed, in the open.
And each time, in the evening lane in Brno, a shy swift
leapt from its hidden branch and made for the sky.

# Dinis Cottage

Behan said there are two things
you don't forget: your first
kiss, your first view of the Killarney
lakes   but there are a thousand

first kisses, you are fourteen
a thousand times, lying in the long-
grassed field exchanging with a boy thirteen
the first unmasking kiss of affection

but Killarney is once I grant you
its waving moist green grasses
godly and long-imagined
and the lake at Muckross was

blue, a blue not spectacular or dazzle
but merely beautiful wind-tossed
water and perfect, and further
into the Muckross woods

at a point where the road wheels
back around toward Killarney
was a low dark cabin shop
where a woman lived alone

where you could set down your bike
indulge in chocolates and sweet drinks
bought off the long dark counter
and pass the slowly-passing time of day

with her and if I could give this
to you   place it in the reach
of your remembering oh then better
than the world or riches I could give you

# Folly

Everything is folly except
for loving God.  So Peig
Sayers said, the last of
many centuries' people of
the Blaskets.  As
she wrote she did not
know her loved isle
would soon be empty,
desolate of talk and
folk; knowing it would
not have changed her
words.  The needing
and crying flesh, the
heart and its hard
wants; her words
have been a stay
against these being
all; her words, the
nothing-weighted air.

# Memento

On the bus through Spiddal,
full car, mostly tourists,
and every mother's son of us
filthy, third-day clothing,
greasy hair and everyone
eyeing the other appreciatively.
The exposed skin in Spiddal is
really ghastly, sweating
beneath our coats, dirt
of the grave on us already,
but still the furtive glance
sneaks across some other's
provocative flesh.  Love
is in the air.  A man wondered
once how the island might even
be populous.  Let me clue you
on that one, bud.  Cold and wet
is sexy.  Death is sexy.
On the bus to Spiddal *I* fell
out of myself and became *we*.

# A Tree on Inishmor,

so wuthered its trunk bends
to permanent west, its leaves
begin in green well above
where branches breach the
trunk.  Obeisance its trick,
it stands.  It leaves leaning
east against the wind to us.

# Epithalamion

*for Tierney and Andy*

Even wool and woven things
you can corrupt, trick
into foolish shapes. But wood
rests incorrupt: ill-carved,
ill-painted, what remains is the
visible life, the dignity beneath
of grain and bark and gnarl.
Scarred, there is whorl and pith.
Be those and build of wood.

# His Wife

We lived knowing the day would come,
but not when, counting down
but to an unknown figure, to infinity.
The day it came it seemed too soon,
policemen crashing in the door, gelignite
and wiring seized in evidence.
You never think it'll be today,
being met by a pair of strangers,
being told, "Robert's been taken,"
hustled without my things out of the country
to this cruddy and forsaken village.
Where, I'm told, I'm immune, though
immune's not what I feel.  You see,
I never spliced a wire, never left a bomb,
never even loaded a gun.
It doesn't mean I don't hate you,
every toadying little smug one of you.
I just couldn't convince myself
you and I were different.
He could believe it.
And he could believe that bombing
a few of you into next week
might do some good.  So we argued
for a lot of our time together.
I pleaded for you: pleaded for every one
of you. Your rights, your limbs,
your babies, your lives.

# The Annunciation, Gerard David, 1490

Northern in its cleanliness and order:
the blue drapings on the bed and the
homely Virgin cloaked in blue;
the *prie-Dieu*, the vase sprouting
its single frond of lily, and a dove,
of all things, descending in aureole;
these sights a thousand of the
imagination's miles from the stark
light of Jerusalem; like the
incongruous angel, white-robed and
barefoot, who flutters with transfiguring
news into the Dutch and unexpecting room.

# Back to Work

The shepherds look older than they are,
always: one weathered face, mustached
and stubbled, looks thirty and is nineteen:
the sheep or the dogs or the farm,
always something. After the storm
the river ran beery and high and
one lamb and then another bumbled in
and commenced to drown itself in the current's
rush: sheep are as stupid as turkeys.
Two waitresses, two maids
and the laundry girl raced about dancing
on the hotel side of the river; three
shepherds and a ghillie hot-footed it
down from the meadow. Archie
who looks thirty raced along in old
rubber boots and dirty pants and dirty coat.
He leapt to the river's edge, pulled one lamb
out sopping, hind legs first. The shepherds
splashed downstream, and Archie ducked
below the high bank, out of sight.
Then the second lamb was pitched into sight,
pausing a white moment in mid-air
like some dripping wingless angel.
He set down in a squishy patch of moss
and scrambled to his feet and baaed
and ran to mother. The other sheep baaed
along, the usual bleat. We clapped and
whistled but Archie strode away,
too used to the urgent customs of the flock
to note applause. He'd seen it, he'd see it
again. The river rushed on and the hills
were huge around us, same as always.

# Sheep

Meet one on the moor and see in its gaze
the twin emotion, anger-born-of-fear:
it'd get you if it weren't afraid.
And it could, in the right corner:
the hard skull-head, exfoliate
from the fleece-cloud of its body,
is hard enough to break bones,
butting your hands or ribs against
the stone wall to protect its young;
its teeth, that you imagine munching
grass, can bite flesh, its hooves
that tap crossing the paved road
can stamp on fingers and will snap them
in a mothering rage.

But on any given Wednesday,
any time but the rare mishap,
they are the thousandfold
brainless herd of the skittish.
The time they can sadden you is
the first night the herds are sorted out,
in the weeks before dipping and shearing:
the young penned off, in Altnaharra,
past and beyond the schoolhouse,
the rams and mothers further around,
over down by the hotel.
That night—before annoyance sets in
and you roll your eyes at the din—
all you hear all night are the cries of the sheep,
the mothers and the young penned apart,
all night crying and crying,

and who of us who have carried and buried
in the unnoticing ground of memory
all this miserable century's images
of fences and separation,
the reaching hands' failed attempts to touch,
will not wish, if only for a moment,
to be away that night,
to carry off (or try)
our fool last image of innocence,
the frolic lamb, to safety?

# For Joyce Rankin

iii.   At Clava,
       we stepped into the stones'
       old cairns and circles, and
       stopped thought to hear
       the stones suggesting where
       to stand, often a little off
       of center, hobbled
       with one foot on a bump of
       ground and the other not,
       amazed what the stones could
       say, did say, hearing this
       each and breaking
       silence to tell
       the other, shored then
       by it a little and ever
       against doubt.

iv.  Even from work came songs.
     I'd read this and assumed
     it meant the old days, spinning
     songs and rowing songs.  But
     even there, at the stainless steel
     sink scrubbing spuds and the pots
     and pans 'til their aluminum
     was bright (at the Hotel
     Altnaharra, Altnaharra, near
     Lairg) we'd get up our own
     daft tunes, the Venison Burger
     Song or the Fish Ditty (on
     Mondays when the fish came in
     from Lairg) or have Michael
     and Maggie rolling their eyes
     at the fourth chorus of Lord
     Won't You Buy Me a Color TV,
     the bunch of us giddy by that
     time, full of the inebriating
     word.  Send me such words,
     dear friend, or sing:  you're
     further north than I am and
     even here the nights are chill.

# La poire d'Anjou

The conjure of its pale green
sunny skin, and the pale green's
pale slight mottle, to evoke the
Anjou pear, *la poire d'Anjou*,
won't do, hovering in mid-air
as the pear then will do: better
to set the heft of it with a
slight blump of the table
(blump the sound the landing
pear makes, you know) on the
black low table, picked out
in gold, better, but not
complete; not even a pear
in the mouth will do, chalky
if left too long on the branch
but rightly both crisp and
dribbly; not even to set
the entire landscape of
Anjou behind the just-
plucked pear, to bear out
its freedom, its stolen,
portable and roadworthy
nature, pitching away the
rind of evidence and planting
*la poire d'Anjou* as you go;
no, to those of right mind
the Anjou pear is Lawrentian
and erotic, its low bulbous
shape sacred and naked,
a shape like the shop-ladies'
thick hips in Le Marais, when you
think at the sight of the Anjou
pear of women's hips you begin
to have it, you have it

almost, but when having an
Anjou pear in hand you flood
with remembering, when the whole
wet sunny landscape of Anjou
comes to you of itself and not
from conjuring, when you are
struck dumb in the market thinking
of the slender young German who
shared with you his just-plucked
pear and walked with you,
and the wet smoothness of its
flesh recalls the bump of his
small bicep, nestled in your hand's
affection and caress, there, oh there
and only then you have it, the
succulent and gorgeous *poire d'Anjou.*

# Mont St. Michel

*for Graham*

First, the mists of distance,
out of which the island swells,
and the tides, the certainties of which
are lunar.  Then face the battlements,
the stones in the bay, face the narrow
shadowed streets, stone too, that wind
around and up; climb the steps
to the ramparts, facing up
past the ebbing tides, and past
the angled stone of wall and tower,
past the green of the garden
even, look where they dreamed to go:
at Michael, who is slender and winged,
bright and absurdly gold,
who swings the sword up, balanced
as a dancer, his toes pressing down
the dragon, Michael who touches earth,
the spire's tip, only a moment.
We do not wait, expectant, to see
the sword sing down and the
dragon slain:  no need:  we bless
our luck instead, to take away
the memory of Michael on the spire's tip,
to have seen him knit for an instant
to the earth, the sword swung up,
the gesture resolute above the tides.

# Chartres

There among the aisles and chapels
it still goes on, the old life,
amidst the medieval racket
of post cards and sacred crockery,
the gabbled cloud of foreign tongues
and people peering at dark corners;
the old life persists, mostly among the old;
the woman leaning to kiss the Virgin's brocaded hem;
the murmur of the devout; white candles
and the clink of francs in the mission box.
A boy of eighteen knelt before the altar,
his face hid in his hands, the muddle
of the life outside pursuing him here as well.

For gems, the painted glass, and for choirs
the figures carved in stone;
Chartres stood their sketch of Paradise,
the place where, as best it could on earth,
time stopped.  It was to be,
as an arch gives stone the power of flight,
the place where faith would give
the clay of flesh its flight, a semblance
whose stones would tug the heart towards prayer,
build in it the desiring of heaven.

I saw the boy again.  At the west door,
beneath the rose of the Judgement,
he met a friend and took him to the font.
He put his fingertips in the holy water
and with them dripping made the sign of the cross
on the body of his friend:
touched his forehead first, the flat of his chest,
the left shoulder, then the right, and last
the slight swell of his belly.

The other in turn, fingers wetted,
touched the forehead of his friend, the chest,
left shoulder and right shoulder
and belly.  They turned to go,
the bead mark of water on their brows.

And when I knelt before the altar,
I prayed:  abject as any man is
in the weight of his faults, scanted
of hope, but who had seen at least the image
of what he desired:  another like himself,
whose flesh he might inscribe
with the water of blessing.

# Winchester

In the crypt below Winchester
Cathedral, its floors and the figure's feet
covered nine months of the year
with water from the Hampshire marshes,

the statue, a late addition, human
in form but undraped
of costume's century or place,
naked in this of sect,

bare in its flesh as we are
in our unmythed thought,
stands with arms crooked and head
bent as if to its book of prayer

and surely only our unfancied time
prevents us naming it The Dreamer
for in my dream the church now
arches up from the figure's thought,

the immensive length of nave and
chantries and Norman stone
still soaring, boss and screen
and glass, but emanate

of the dreamer in the crypt,
marsh-footed figure of creating,
always there surely but only in
our human-dreaming time remembered.

# In England

Who was I ever to assume
I would live settled among
my things, at ease amid
luxury's weight?  Books:

octavos, half-leathers, fine
bindings.  In my sack a
ratty paperback of John
Clare's poems, off a trades
shelf in a Gower Street hotel,

inscribed by someone to a
girl, who'd discarded it.  My
portion, the less and less,
the ever closer to enough.

# For Paul Verlaine

Did you know it before you took the hand
of that mean little blond provincial,
that the end would come as it did,
not Phedre wringing the hushed crowd's heart
with speech, but syphilitic stillness
that has nothing to do but go on?

———————————

Given a clean warm room he threw
his shaming verminous clothes into the street,
greeting, naked, the Parisian crowds below.
When you saw him, golden in the lamplit,
unbargaining act, you knew you could
leave them now, the slippers and knickknacks
of your father-in-law's safe house.
You had a place to go at last.

———————————

He would say: *A toi, toute la vie.*
He would say: *Je veux etre avec toi, je t'aime.*
He would say: *A toi. Je t'attends.*

———————————

Blue eyes shooting arrows at the future,
he stood, a promise in the flesh.
There they were, in reach at last.
The Belgian fields.
The wheat of freedom.

# What the World Is

It comes best as a shock,
I tell you.  The roseate mist
of the Seine:  a road in one life
goes from Jewett City
to the Seine.  I never expected that.

Small sorrows go on as well.
By starlight, hitching past the flat fields
of Normandy, one may be clutched
by a small fear in the vitals
to be so far from home,

but, going backwards down the road,
thumb out, see the light of St. Michel,
become an island late that evening,
a star fallen but blazing still,
and be shaken such light exists.


And on the Seine a small prison-like
concrete room, and two hundred
thousand small lights:  the Memorial
to the Jews deported from Paris

to the death camps:  imagine two
hundred thousand lights, the burnt flesh
that means, the molested lives.
What the world is, we did not suspect.

# Evening Rites

i.   Where we have danced for so long
    (the old dance—hands held, a circle

    of twelve souls, the altar dance
    in the suttas) that the summer grass

    is matted with our tracks, dusk
    succeeding the long glare of midday,

    where now, crowded inside the circle,
    the chanting and laughter done, the voices

    one by one fallen still, we stand and wait
    to see the evening star.

ii.   At the round stone table,
at night. Or almost night,
the streaked sky. Bats
scammering by, and "bats,"
someone says, noticing
them. Grapes in bunches,
and a loaf, an end-piece
already cut and eaten.
Four of us at table,
the puzzle of it clear
on our faces; the cows
lowing in the field,
as though uncertain,
as though we are not
alone; which we are
not, and never were.

iii.    Bring me the bare branch,
unflowering.  Set the dirtshod
stone in my hand, and go.
This last of rites I enact
alone.  You and you, at
the wood's edge, peering
in, will guard me.  When
I emerge again alone,
then speak.  The bare
branch, unflowering, and
the stone, still cold
to touch:  call these good,
against the heart's cry
for luxury.

# Hearing the Dalai Lama

*New York, August 1999*

I don't remember much of what he said.
I remember Dan telling us at lunch
of being in Laos decades before,
watching from a hill
two lines of soldiers firing at each other,
and the sudden silence
as a line of Theravadan monks
crossed the field between them,
walking with bowls and lowered heads into town
to beg for lunch, and how the soldiers
started in shooting again after they'd passed.

The talk was complicated, a commentary
on the practices of a bodhisattva.
I remember the expectant silence in the theatre,
teens in knee-ripped jeans next to the ladies
with Gucci bags, people offering their seats
to older folks.  We stood

and the D.L. strolled onstage,
ordinary in monk's robes, climbed
the teaching throne and motioned to us to sit.
Then he puttered.  Got settled,
adjusted robes, laid out wide pages of text,
took his watch off and set it where he could see it.
Then he adjusted his robes some more.
This went on for minutes
with the hush in the theater thick as wool.
Then he cocked his eye at us, shifted pages again,
and let off a coy little chirrup whistle,
hum-dum, tum-ti-dum-dum, here I am,

I'm going to teach Eternal Wisdom,
be with you in a minute. And the place,
as they say, came down.
Then we settled in and listened.

Hours later, mentally sand-blasted and
somnolent in the warm August theatre,
we were asked to stand for a blessing.
He spoke as he had in Tibetan;
it sounded like Japanese and French mixed up.
I don't know what that other silence was,
before and after, distinct and unheard,
but you don't need it explained, do you?
It was a good thing not to hear.

# What is it the Buddha says

of time, yes, the kalpas,
the eon that, a robin passing
once in a thousand years
and the feather of its evening
wing brushing a touch
of dust from Sumeru's peak,
would be as long as
Sumeru took to vanish.

A blessing to be pulled as
long as nature's patience;
to see, beyond the thick building
of our time, past the ungenerous
and agreed commands, a green
that will outgrow them, a mass
of living overthrow.

# Story

It becomes the way you see,
listen, size things up:
rapid, with bits not fully
explained, song or sentence
in mid-phrase, the movie
you've sat down to midway.
Just the people, everyday:
who is George the woman
spoke of, the tale the lady
tells you because you're friendly,
it's all had its running start
long before and it's left ground,
it's in mid-air, a flung pebble.
Weft and nexus of stories,
each person, contact with another
one thread of its point of plot,
flexion as a third person touches
and a fourth, past persons to
light, to wind, the wood-scent
of winter fires, the stories
indoor around them, 'til any
stepping out is into its
headlong, its myriad, its going-on.

# Whitman, and the Gay Thing

Sophistication, become mere habit,
brittles into a stance of knowing
'til sinews, blood, heart, the height
of hope, parch into ironies.  The love
of comrades, Whitman called it:
we know what that means, don't we,
dear?  But you don't, you know.  In
Calamus, those poems, I found a kind of
father's text, that tells us in blunt
rapt words, thank God, that we too
must give up our jests at last
and go out on the road,
poor men, to the starred sky and
rain, must risk the awful ventures
of loving, or waiting in our lives
unloved; that we too, man and boy,
must take it straight.

# Somewhere

I think of my father asleep in his hospital room.
His life is ending, running down, running out.
I think of his wife, my mother, dead these twenty years,
and his second wife, no longer young herself.
My friends are living out their lives somewhere,
some west, some south, Cape Breton, Lazenay.
I remember the Buddhist monks, a clique of them
in New York, saffron and maroon robes and
the black-grit streets, American, most of them,
their excited chatter. The long, slow hours
of night go by. Izumi Shikibu, a thousand years ago,
begged the moon for its light and guidance.

# The Moon

A bit at a time, and a bit more,
I leave my dream, I'm back in my body, awake.
The dark shapes sort themselves, my room
at home, 2.20 morning by the clock.
I'm weighted, sopped, breathing heavy in the panic
of deep night.  What brought me—
but then I know, the shade's pulled back
in the chill room, and the silver spherical
bright full moon illumines the yard, unseemly light.
The pear tree, utterly still and counting:
how many years alone, how many more?
The German Shepherd two houses down
barking in fury, not at a burglar but at the moon:
why should the dark be shown so clearly?
why should he be made to feel like this?

# Up Knocknarea

*for Tim Russell*

Carry a stone and place it on Maeve's cairn, they said,
and be blessed in love, the lucky man of all,
relief of dreaded bachelordom the reward;

and so we did (you carried a bigger stone than I)
knowing it a ploy to keep the tourists
from carrying the whole thing piece by piece away

but happy, walking the road to Carrowmore,
to play even the mock of custom, content
to give invented blessing its chance to work.

And so it did, though in the usual left-field way
of Ireland; we puffed our way up the top
of Knocknarea, from there climbed up Maeve's cairn,

and there it was, around us, the strain and pull
of the muscles in our eyes to see so far,
more of green lands that we'd ever hoped could be,

the white of towns and, to the east of us, Ben Bulben,
set down in vaster stonepoint sprawl
than the dream of flying things could compass,

and wind, that if I'd opened up my coat
you might've had to hold with our doubled weights
the only hope of keeping me on earth.

This way Maeve blessed us, and if love this month
comes knocking, to offer us the role of tender spouse,
we might not now be the right men for the job:

up Knocknarea a something undomestic
fledges and strikes home: the war queen's gift,
her keeping you, such that a wife would find us

too unhearthed and strange, a pair of plough-slips,
would grieve when that cold green gaze got loose again,
a silence she'd know inviolable and unsought.

# Glendalough

Down the path to the holy well
and down the way through trees
I walked easily away
from the century's disbelief.

In the unroofed chapel alone
with the cold stones' welcome
prayer leapt to my lips
like a freshet breaking ground

speaking 'til, like the saint's card left
on the mullioned sill, I was framed
by the little church to quiet, to hear
like tides rising to the heart's sense

the stride of Christ, like a giant
in a tale, heart-hammering, come
thunder stilly down the path, fetch
all up in it like a windruck

and pass, setting the ghost
of me to ground again, safe
in the stones' welcome yet,
housed in a wild silence.

# The Flowering

I love to imagine London fallen quiet,
silent really, just past the toll of twelve;
walking past the white bulk of St. Paul's
or by the steps of Paternoster Square;
not in the panicked silences of nights
of the Blitz but merely unpeopled streets,
London asleep, lit bright by the moon,
quiet as the pond and woods behind our house.
I stroll down Fleet Street in my dreaming
to peer in the dark alleys and entries
that lead to the Inns of Court; a stray dog
may stroll by but of even the police
I hear no more than their echoing talk.
Up the curl of Goodge Street I lay my
hand flat in affection on the stout black
door of Johnson's house, and as in my
night the church is lit, I enter
the sadness of St. Dunstan's, its
silences like the streets outside. In
the short night of a poem I reach
Trafalgar Square, still lit, like an
etching, by the moon, unpeopled yet
even by lovers; then pale dawn edges up
and people appear, morning-eyed, stepping
from their dreams to speech, and like
them I take coffee in the crypt below
St. Martin's. I watch them, the creatures
of a city I have dreamed, the flowering
of an ache to be at home and there,
and they vanish up the bustle of
Charing Cross or past the fruit market
at Villiers Street, they vanish as I start
awake to other thoughts, or fall past
them in the peace of dreaming.

# An Incident on the Street

It did happen, in London in 1921
near Staple Inn, off Holborn.
A woman reading on a bench
beneath a plane tree felt a tremor
and looking up saw that the pavement
once before her had quite quietly
disappeared. She stood
and looked into the freshmade gap
and saw, some twenty feet below,
her own face peering back.

The well, some centuries old,
had made a break for daylight.
So might we all some day.
And the woman, she insisted
to the Times, was not in the least
upset. Whatever happens to us
but ourselves?

# Arriving in China

Just turned as we arrive:
it's now Year of the Golden Pig,
and Shenzhen is adorned:
pictures of pigs, posters of pigs,
pigs on pillars, pigs on parade,
pigs pigs pigs. It's an auspicious
year for babies: government says
have only one, but tradition whispers:
have it now. I'm overcome, giggly,
euphoric, and pigs to you, mama,
my heart of hearts babbles. Have a
big piggy year. May your children
swill richly of the heart's, the world's,
the spirit's goods. Pig out.

# A Chastening

In the Lichee Park, Spring's
in its warm riot, an orchestra's
rehearsing, strollers rolling
past the rough-barked palms
and characters carved on stones.
Folks nod to us, three
westerners.  In the shade we pass
a middle-aged lady who's
written calligraphy in water
on the walk, gracile forms
almost vanishing as they dance.
We know to bow to her,
and she accepts it.  I blush
to think of poets boasting
to be immortal.

# Yamdroktso

We drove 'round it
like a moth around light,
up the ochre steeps

of Kambla, midday
as clear to us
as error made right.

Miles of folding shore
down in the rattling van
to drive along it, chasing

them, the storied turquoise
waters, wild to see more of
the wind-roughed slopes

(where dark-dreaming hands
at work, filthying a sacred
lake, labor when I sleep)

of the threatened edge, we knew,
of the cleanly world,
wise and delighting.

# Light

Seeking the most beautiful sun-
light in the world will lead you
into Lhasa. Bah I say to the
sandy beaches, Barbados, such-
like. The splendor of sun you
see only in Lhasa. Believe.

Mere men of science tell you
Lhasa, all Tibet, is made up
of so many million tons of
this or that stone. But I say
Lhasa, all Tibet, is made of
light entirely. Look.

Up the broad and steep and
innumerable steps of the
Potala (eleven hundred rooms
but no one has counted or
will ever count all the steps)

out of the dark and gold-filled
chambers, you remember the term
"emptiness" is our rendering
of "sky-like mind," the blue
clear unobstruction you go into.
Look. Everywhere. Light.

# It Is All So Simple

We are in the Barkhor, as strange to them
as they to us.  The hot day sun in Lhasa
takes off our hats and scarves and quilted shirts.
People exit the Jokhang, having crossed fields
and plains and rivers and vast ranges of peaks
to come for the New Year.  They grin widely
at the four of us, the only westerners in sight.
An ancient woman swathed in a black coat
beelines to me, walks beside me a few steps
and pats my arm.  "Tashi delek," she says, her
greeting, and we walk a ways, my hand on hers.
She has six teeth and gives me the world.  It was what
I'd come for, unknowing.  It is all so simple.

# Tientaishan

After the bright dust-blown light,
the tumult wind, Gyantse, Yamdroktso,
Lhasa, now to dappled Spring, Hangzhou.
The dew-wet pale green leaves
on the silver-white trunks of bamboo.
Roused out at oh-dark-hundred by
a monk clapping hard blocks of wood.

Still dawnlike skies, the still
courtyard, before the steamed bread
and rice and mushrooms for breakfast.
The getting-up noises from the monks'
rooms.  I'm out on the porch, taking in
the shining sloped rooves of the
temple, the little shop that sells
incense and malas and buddhas
and monk's shoes.  Eaves-sparrows
taking cracker crumbs off the rail.

Mr. Lin drives us up to Cold Mountain
talking of his son, now almost as
tall as himself, through the terraced
hills of Hangzhou, farmed a thousand
years this way.  We leave the lower
caves with the weathered altars and
voices chanting the name of Amitabha,
walk and climb the old trails

afoot to the topmost cave.  Han-shan
here wrote out his record of a life,
some of it desperate poor and sad,
some of it moonlit and at ease.
A nun here has inherited his silence,
his place away, and lives spiking
down the stony floor of the cave,
smoothing it so visitors will not fall.

Without a word she makes us welcome,
pressing a sheaf of tracts into our hands.
From the dark frame of the cave
the hills look lustrous and calm.
We make our bows at the altar,
leave an offering; our friend is
back at work before we leave.
And a bright plumed bird whose name
I'll never know sings us the way back.

# Monte Irago: Cruz de Ferro

They look like a pile of skulls, the stones.
In the deep of them are stones the Celts left,
then Romans. The hermit Gaucelmo raised
a high spindle of wood and an iron cross.
You leave the stone there you've carried
from Roncesvalles. You leave the stone, the photo,
the linen, the scarf. You have to leave them,
they are of the life behind you: the sorrows
that were like swarms of bees on the lone days,
crossing La Meseta. Like the ivy of a love.
You begin to tear yourself away then, but
still, at the last: how hard to leave them.

# Casa Machado

In Segovia. Of the palaces and hills,
as I'm sure someone has said. Of Romanesque
*conventos*. In the shadowed alley
off the Marques del Arco, the little house
shimmers in the world of the spirit. Here
Machado lived, the poet. Great
in its tiny rooms. The woman (who has
worked here only a day) opens the door
to his bedroom. Like an unveiling. She knows.
Here the foaming breakers of Love fell
roughly. Here a seedling, Life, reached
for its expression in the air. Here Death
drew back his talons. Briefly. They were giants,
even their softest talk would shatter our ears.
In these rooms they moved at their comfort.
They had come to ask the master for human words.
He listened, intent. Later, with his pen,
alone in the poor rooms again. Began.

# A Phrase from Homer

And at the end, before he died,
what struck him, last
of his mortal thoughts, was the phrase
he'd read in Homer, the warrior
with his throat pierced
by a spear: "And his eyes then
filled with darkness." The tide
of black, the old poet precise
about even that. Then the darknesses
behind him and before him met,
and he was gone.

# The Lucky One

The desk with its empty wooden bowl
and bottle of cough syrup and tea-tin
full of change; the slope garret
ceiling, the wooden walls and few books,
my room you visited the once.  I send you
these for the good they've been to me.
To hold hope for a little
near the breast is good; even
the husky words of farewell or
separation can be good; I was
the lucky one who held you dear.
Hoist sail! or drive on:
even of our few words, given
who spoke them, nothing is waste.

# Spring Snow, Connecticut

The gander, his back laddered with white,
picks his way disgusted across the cold lawn.
The Buddha's birthday,
the clocks turned forward for April:
incense in the chill room.
Snow from a sky bright still at six
hushes the buds of apple.
The monk bows and asks: "What is the Pure Land?"
The teacher says: "Who has defiled you?"

# The Tokaido Road

Oh, long years! Yes, long!
Or many, perhaps, not long.
Up and down, up and down
the Tokaido road, begging
for enough to live, sleeping
as the guest of strangers.
Writing on strips of cloth
NAMU AMIDA BUTSU, giving
them to passers-by. Give
what you own away, my
teacher said, then look up
at the night full of stars.
Nephew, I am dying. My life
has been good. This is
my farewell to you.

# Night

If later we lied—lied to parents,
lied to neighbors, lied to friends—
call it payback for the filth
they fed us, the names they gave
to what we did. That night
in the moon-regarded house
we were grave and kind. What
could the other's being clumsy matter,
if only we both were there?
When a neighbor's dog barked
at the window we like child-kings
opened it and gave him bread.

# The Privacies of Light

Everyone has their own, I hope,
the privacies of light, mere things
illumined. Just the word "saunter,"
for instance, on the pages of Thoreau,
is heroic light to me, gravity
undone; a Norwegian ten-kroner
coin, found at the Tuileries,
when I handle it, never does not
delight me: a crossroad
of nations, avouched me in
the Paris dirt. The grace of age
must be in this pile-up of
bright privacies, the light-
hoard: a certain bench in
the close at Winchester, where
one may hum (and I have)
the hymn of Blake's Jerusalem:
the green lands of one's
gathering, the events of mercy.

# Worse than Anything

*for Joyce Rankin*

Because, because habit, you see,
so easily overwhelms us.
It grows like a caul
over all we see with, feel with,

shivers and runs numb
the thin line we connect with.
So I distrust possessions,
I chafe at home, at title

and plenty.  Our Highland days
and after, loose in London,
living eager out of backpacks
and pinching apples off the trees

in Embankment Park:  fair seed-time
and harvest both, the little we had.
I love the unpetty spirits that loomed
in us, healing with tears old griefs

that opened us to be bound fast
as friends.  What could years be
to the time that taught us that worse
than anything is the cold, unbroken heart.

GLENN SHEA was born and has lived most of his life in Connecticut. He has worked in the library of a cancer clinic and in the French department of a foreign-language bookshop, washed dishes in the Scottish Highlands, gone to pilgrim's mass in Santiago and eaten really good Tex-Mex in Chengdu. He has read his poetry in venues ranging from the Harvard Divinity School to Shakespeare and Company in Paris. He is living for the moment in an old farmhouse in Uncasville and works with a group of illuminati in a huge used-book shop in Niantic, Connecticut. He has published two chapbooks. *Find A Place That Could Pass For Home* is his first full-length collection.

**salmon**poetry**40**

*Publishing Irish & International Poetry Since 1981*

# The Salmon Bookshop & Literary Centre

Ennistymon, County Clare, Ireland

"Another wonderful Clare outlet."
*The Irish Times*, 35 Best Independent Bookshops